# THE TIDY GUIDE TO WRITING A NOVEL

The clutter-free, 30-minute course for writing your book
right the first time

___

## RACHEL AUKES

WAYPOINT BOOKS

## The Tidy Guide Series by Rachel Aukes

*The Tidy Guide to Writing a Novel*

**Coming Soon:**

*The Tidy Guide to Self-Editing Your Novel*

*The Tidy Guide to Publishing a Novel*

# Contents

**WAYPOINT BOOKS**

THE TIDY GUIDE TO WRITING A NOVEL

Cover Design by Evernight Designs.

Print ISBN-13: 978-1-7328449-1-9

# Introduction

To write is to adopt an exciting, self-driven lifestyle where you have the opportunity to create characters that readers fall in love with and build worlds that readers want to live in.

Writing a novel can be both the most rewarding and the most intimidating experience you face in your life. To finish a novel is a huge accomplishment, and no major accomplishment comes easy. A novel is a layered symphony of worldbuilding, character development, dialogue, narrative, and much more. It's easy to get lost. Many people who start writing a book never finish. I've met writers who've been working on their first novel for years, some longer than a decade. I've talked with many more who have bits and pieces of a novel sitting in a drawer, collecting dust.

I find these unfinished dreams a tragedy. It's one thing to decide that you no longer wish to write a book, but if you still dream of writing one, having an unfinished manuscript will always weigh on your spirit and confidence. It's time to finish that novel.

I spent years dreaming of writing a novel. I'd written plenty of short stories when I was a child, and I continued to dabble in short fiction into adulthood. I'd jot down story ideas, but I never started a novel, not even a few words. Writing a book was this colossal mountain that I had no idea how to climb. How in the world could I write a 300-page tome when I'd never written more than fifteen- or twenty-page stories in my life? Then one day, I grabbed my laptop and typed a scene that had kept going through my mind. I'd first thought it'd be a short story, but after reading my words, I realized the scene would fit perfectly with an idea I had for a book.

On that day, I began my first novel, *Knightfall*. Some days, I'd write a few pages. Other days, nothing. I got stuck a lot, and I had to rewrite *a lot*. Writing a novel was exhausting, but it was also fun. It wasn't until after I'd written two more novels that I realized how much time and energy I'd wasted on my first book by not applying any kind of structured process to my writing.

I spent sixteen months writing my first book. Now, after having over a dozen novels published, I can write a novel in a month. I've certainly improved my craft, but what's made the biggest difference is that I apply a repeatable, decluttered approach to each story.

I'm now a full-time writer, but I wrote the first twelve books while working full-time as a change agent. I helped companies declutter their processes and environments by cutting anything that didn't bring value—i.e., the unnecessary work—and then devising plans to ensure that they'd see continual improvements in how they worked.

The funny thing is that I'd applied these concepts to all facets of my life except writing. At home, I'd decluttered my house using a blend of my training and the KonMari Method, which also applies the same concept of cutting everything that doesn't bring value (with KonMari, you cut everything that doesn't bring joy). I considered myself an efficiency expert until I looked at my writing habits and saw that I was anything but efficient. I had convinced myself that decluttering rules didn't apply to a creative endeavor like writing.

I was so very wrong.

When I applied decluttering concepts, such as cutting time-wasters and planning my work in advance, I discovered that I was writing faster and producing higher quality books. Now, I never have to go back and rewrite a scene because something I wrote in Chapter Twenty-Three contradicts what happens in Chapter Three. I write with more enthusiasm and self-assurance than ever before.

In this Tidy Guide—just thirty minutes of reading— I'll show you clutter-free steps to planning and writing so that you can confidently write your novel right the first time. And, I'll show you how you can avoid hitting walls, such as the ultimate procrastination excuse known as writer's block, by achieving Little Ups every day.

Embrace the adventure!

ONE

# Why is writing a novel so hard?

## Write your book right the first time

This guide focuses on writing a novel, which is "a fictitious prose narrative of book length, typically representing character and action with some degree of realism" (Dictionary.com). A novel may fit into a genre, such as romance, science fiction, mystery, or thriller. Or it may not fit neatly into any genre, in which case it's labeled general, literary, or mainstream fiction. It may also be directed at a specific age group, such as adults, young adults, or children. This guide applies to all types of novels, though each genre has its own rules that I'll mention later.

Inside the publishing industry, book length is determined by word count. Generally, a novel is at least 40,000 words. Anything shorter is considered a novella (17,500–39,999 words), a novelette (7,500–17,499 words), or a short story (fewer 7,500 words). One page usually has 250–300 words; however, fonts, font sizes, and margins can drastically change the actual number of words on a page, and therefore, the number of pages in a book. This is why writers, agents, editors, and publishers all speak in terms of word count rather than the number of pages.

This guide focuses on novels, though you can apply the same principles to novellas and novelettes. Short stories are written differently since you're packing a complete story in a condensed package. If you're writing a non-fiction book, the rules are significantly different, so we'll cover that type of book in a separate Tidy Guide.

In this guide, I'll show you five straightforward steps you can take to plan your novel. I've pared down the steps to the activities that will bring you the most value in writing your book without delaying getting started. How deep you take each step is up to you, but if you spend time on each step, you'll find that you'll stay focused on the most important activity of all—WRITING—and not get lost along the way.

If you've already started writing your novel, take a break to read through the five planning steps. This will give you time to reflect on your overall story. If you've been floundering, these five steps will get you back on track and energized to continue writing your novel.

The steps need not take long. You can spend one session to go through all five steps at once, or you can break out the steps into multiple sessions. For example, you may focus on your characters one time and then on your world another time. You can go through the steps alone or with a partner. How you perform the steps is up to you.

When you write your novel, you'll come to appreciate the planning process and the clarity it gives you.


## Make "Little Ups" your motto

Once you go through the five planning steps to ensure you write your book right the first time, you'll be ready (and excited) to begin writing. Writing is both the easiest and most intimidating part of being a writer. That's why so many writers start novels but never finish.

Here's where the concept of Little Ups comes in. Little Ups are small but very real achievements, and I'll show you how to use them to keep writing and slam through writer's block. Each Little Up gives you a sense of accomplishment and brings you one step closer to finishing your novel. For each writing session, you'll set a Little Up goal. Examples of a Little Up are:

- Write 100 words
- Write one page
- Write a complete scene
- Finish a chapter
- Write for 60 minutes without interruption
- Write something six days per week
- Read a chapter you've written
- Post a chapter on Wattpad

The first Little Up for any new book is to give it a working title. Once you give your book a name, you give it an identity. Every person has a name, and your book is important enough to have one, too. If you haven't already, give your novel a title and celebrate the Little Up. Introduce your book to the world by writing the title on a piece of paper and then displaying it with pride.

You're already one step closer to writing the novel. Worried that the title may need to change once you start writing? That's fine. You can always change the title later.

Use Little Ups as milestones to motivate you to stay focused. Writers, as a general lot, tend to be too hard on themselves. Little Ups help you recognize that you are making progress, even when it feels like every word you need is buried deep in a sludge pit. On those days, achieving a Little Up, no matter how small, is a great leap forward.

## Write with the pen, edit with the sword

If you try to make your first draft a worldwide bestseller, you'll get frustrated and never finish. There's a time and place for everything. First, write the story. Get it down on paper (or, on the screen, more likely). Make notes regarding any changes that need made as they come to mind. Maybe you need to look up the year Napoleon marched on Waterloo, or you think you changed your protagonist's eye color. Jot down the note and move on. Don't let the "to do's" get in the way of your momentum. There will be plenty of time to fix things when you have the first draft completed.

Then, you can improve the story during the editing process. When you self-edit, you cut unnecessary parts, such as the infamous "day in the life" scenes. On my first book, I cut two entire chapters because they didn't move the story forward. Editing can be a difficult yet fulfilling experience, because it's all about making your novel the best book it can be.

I've seen a few writers take the changes personally, believing (incorrectly) that the edits are a reflection of the author and not of the story. They've grown so attached to their story that they don't want to cut a single word. I can understand—those words took a lot of time and energy to write. The key to a good edit is to not take edits personally. No story is perfect. It doesn't matter if you're J. K. Rowling, Stephen King, or a first-time novelist, everyone's story needs edited.

As part of the publishing process, you should work with

an editor on your novel. However, there are many things you can do as an author to self-edit and polish your novel that will make working with an editor so much easier. In *The Tidy Guide to Self-Editing Your Story*, I give you a variety of checks and assessments that you can perform on your novel to make it your personal best.

## Don't underestimate the noise of life

Life gets in the way. Whether you're in school, have a job, or have a family, other priorities will demand your time and energy. The key to writing your novel is to determine where that fits into your life's priorities and then treat it accordingly. Is writing a novel more important than spending time on social media or gaming? Then, make sure you achieve your Little Ups before you go onto Instagram, Snapchat, or Reddit.

You may find it helpful to schedule time to write, just like you would a doctor appointment or a lunch date. By setting aside a block of time on your calendar—and holding yourself to it—you will make progress. If you schedule and write ten minutes every morning, that's over an hour's worth of writing every week. Make each ten-minute sprint a Little Up, and you start the day with a big positive.

TWO

## Plan your novel first

---

### Jumping right in guarantees frustration

When I have a new story idea, I can't wait to start writing. However, I've learned that if I jump right in, I stumble more as I write and have to fix more things later. I save myself a lot of time writing and rewriting with some up-front planning.

Writers are often classified by their writing style. Plotters are writers who thoroughly plan—or plot—their novel ahead of time and work from detailed outlines. Pantsers tend to jump into writing with minimal planning and make it up as they go; in other words, they write from the seat of their pants. I, like most writers, fall somewhere in between the two extremes. I don't plot out every single scene in detail, but I do need to understand major plot points and my characters and the world they live in before I start writing, or else I find that my characters look like cardboard cutouts and world feels flat.

The five steps I cover below gather the information necessary to begin your novel, regardless of your writing style. What varies is how deep you go into each step. For example, when creating characters in step three, a pantser may have only a couple of bullets under their main characters' names, while a plotter may have complete biographies.

The tangible benefit of completing the five steps is that each step requires you to proactively think about a major element of your novel before you begin writing. Otherwise, if you jump right in, you'll encounter frustration in having to go back and rework your novel because you didn't write it right the first time.

Oh, and treat each step as a Little Up, and you'll see that you're making big progress on your novel, even before writing the first paragraph.

## Step 1: Develop a premise you love

When people find out that you're writing a novel, they'll ask, "What's your novel about?" How will you respond?

I see one of two responses from the ill-prepared, and believe me, I've been there myself. I've been guilty of the first response—the blank stare as I think of how I can possibly explain my massive tome to this person, and then I spout out random plot points. The second response is even worse for the poor questioner—the writer drones on and on, giving a full synopsis of the book. Both responses are red flags that the writer doesn't truly understand what their book is about; the writer doesn't understand the **premise**.

The premise is the central idea of your book; it's what makes your novel unique. Premises are often structured either as *What If* statements or as *When* statements.

*What If* statements pose a question and are especially popular in the speculative fiction genres, such as science fiction and futuristic thrillers. These statements focus on an inciting incident, i.e., that which kicks off the main story. For example, the premise of *War of the Worlds* is, "What if hostile Martians landed on Earth?"

*When* statements are popular in romance and general fiction and especially in contemporary fiction. Rather than focusing on a single, big question, *When* statements focus on a narrative, i.e., the general progression of the story. For example, the premise of *Jane Eyre* is, "When a woman becomes a governess, she finds herself in love with the estate's brooding master."

When someone asks, "what's your novel about?" they don't want to hear a full rundown of the plot. They want to hear its premise. In the corporate world, they call a succinct response an elevator speech, which means you should be able to explain whatever it is that needs explained in the time the elevator takes to travel between two floors.

To come up with the premise for your book, you need to do a little brainstorming. Ask yourself questions like these:

- What's the conflict?
- What's the inciting incident?
- What's the story arc?
- What key elements stand out in the storyline?

On a side note, another term that's loosely related to the premise is **logline**. A logline conveys your story in a single, punchy sentence that introduces (1) the protagonist, (2) the antagonist, and (3) the story's stakes. If you are asked to pitch your story to an agent or editor, this is the first thing they want to hear. Here's a rough example for *Star Wars*: A farm boy joins rebel forces to save a princess from an evil Jedi master and the galaxy from a planet-destroying Death Star.

**Conflict** can be external, such as a hero fighting a villain. In my *Fringe Series*, the conflict is an interplanetary war. But conflict can also be internal, focusing on the character's growth through a significant event in his or her life, such as a car accident, death, or a love affair. Many romance stories focus on the internal conflict that keeps the two protagonists from coming easily together.

The **inciting incident** is the event that launches the character(s) into action. In my book, *100 Days in Deadland*, Cash begins a typical day at the office, only to be disrupted by the zombie apocalypse. This is a grand-scale inciting incident, but it doesn't have to be so massive. An inciting incident can also be a character starting their first day of school in a new town. The key to a good inciting incident is its disruption of the protagonist's life.

The **story arc** is the overall progression of your book's narrative. In Tolkien's *The Lord of the Rings*, the story arc is a monumental quest. In my *Fringe Series*, the arc is a fight for independence. Many YA (Young Adult) novels have a coming-of-age story arc.

**Key elements** of the story may be items, objects, or universal themes. In *Snow White and the Seven Dwarfs*, the apple was a key element. In my *Fringe Series*, a key element is the teardrop symbol worn by the torrents. It may be too early to know the key elements of your novel, but if you begin with one in mind, it'll be easier to weave it into the fabric of the story.

Once you've brainstormed these four questions, look at your answers. Creating a premise is much like fitting together a jigsaw puzzle. Play with the different pieces to see which work. Where a premise differs from a puzzle is that you might not use all the pieces, but save them for later. All those extra pieces may help you write your blurb.

Keep the premise to one or two sentences and write it in present tense. Once you have a premise that you find engaging, you can use that as your novel's tagline as you write it.

The next time someone asks you, "What's your novel about?" give them the premise, and they'll be begging for more, which brings all the more motivation to write that novel.

## Step 2: Know your novel's demographics

Step Two is about understanding the demographics, or descriptive categories, your novel fits in. These three demographics will help you from page one to the last page of your novel by giving it confines in which to work.

- Is it a standalone or part of a series?
- What's its genre (and subgenre, if applicable)?
- What's its expected length?

Will your book be a standalone novel, or will it be part of a series? Some standalones can be expanded into a series, especially when each novel within the series stands on its own—think of the James Bond novels. If it's standalone, you may want to consider series potential down the road should you wish to revisit your novel's world again. If you decide your novel will be a part of a series, then you must stay aware of both the story's arc and the series arc as you write.

Another demographic to consider is the genre where your book fits. Genre is important because each genre comes with its own set of rules. Romance always has a

Happily Ever After (HEA), or at least a Happily For Now (HFN), ending and focuses on the relationship of the main characters. Fantasy must include something of the fantastical, while science fiction must contain a sense of plausibility. Westerns are generally set in the Old West prior to the twentieth century. Accurate details are a must in historical fiction, there must be a case to solve in mystery novels, there must be a sense of dread in horror fiction, and there must be an adventure to be found within a thriller. Any genre can also target an age group, such as YA (Young Adult), which targets ages 12-18.

Each genre also has its own subgenre, which may have more specific rules of its own. Just a few subgenres of fantasy include alternate history, urban fantasy, high fantasy, historical fantasy, or dark fantasy. Romance includes contemporary romance, historical romance, paranormal romance, science fiction romance, and many more.

If you're not sure where your novel fits, take a look at books already on the shelves. Based on your story's premise, where does it fit? Then, be sure you've read enough in your genre to know readers' expectations. Genre rules should be never broken, not if you want satisfied readers.

The genre you write in can help dictate how many words you should try to target. For example, fantasy novels tend to be longer than mystery novels. Westerns and category romance (e.g., Harlequin titles) tend to be on the shorter side, sometimes under 50,000 words. If you are interested in publishing with a particular house, be sure to research that publisher's submission guidelines. Each publishing house—and imprint within the house—has rules of its own.

In today's world of e-books, word count is becoming less stringent, but it's still a factor. Don't focus too much on word count; story always trumps word count. Don't pad your novel with words to build up the word count, and don't cut good scenes to shrink your word count. Each story should be as long as it needs to be and no more. Know the rules so if you break them, you do so with intention.

## Step 3: Give your readers characters they can connect with

The first two planning steps focus on the macro pieces of your novel, i.e., "the big picture." The remaining three steps focus on the micro pieces, digging in to three things that will equip you to write your novel with speed while ensuring it has the depth and richness of a classic. The first and most important of these steps focuses on characters.

If your main characters don't feel like real people to you when you begin writing your novel, they won't feel real to your readers. Readers crave characters they can love (or love to hate). To create three-dimensional characters, they need to be more than a name and a physical description. They need to have a *purpose*, *personality*, and *backstory*.

Characters have no place in your novel if they serve no purpose other than for the protagonist to voice their thoughts out loud for the reader's benefit. Every character must have a motivation to move the story forward, whether that is helping or hindering the protagonist's journey. Their roles may appear small at first. Look at the Weasley family in *Harry Potter*: each family member played a role in Harry's progression. Don't think that just because a character is minor you don't need them to feel real. Sometimes, a minor character becomes a fan favorite.

Personality and backstory often go hand in hand, as a character's experiences often shape their behavior and beliefs, and their personality quirks lead them down different paths in life.

In terms of personality, think of the unique traits that shape the character. Arrogant, compassionate, clumsy, unconfident, perfectionistic, compulsive, nomadic, phobic, abusive... the list goes on and on. Pick a trait and think of how it would shape your character's decisions.

Each personality trait can be seen as both a strength and a weakness. For example, the eternal optimist may run into a bad situation without thinking. Or, a compassionate person may become prey to an abuser. As you develop your characters, consider how their traits can create problems for the characters to deal with, past, present, and future.

If your story has a distinct protagonist and antagonist, consider how their personalities play off each other. The protagonist is often the yin to the antagonist's yang.

Too many times, I've seen richly drawn protagonists facing off against cardboard antagonists. This is disappointing because the protagonist's journey often wouldn't be possible without the antagonist's involvement. Give as much attention to creating your antagonist as your protagonist, and you'll find the plot will be deeper and more exciting.

---

*"You don't really understand an antagonist until you understand why he's a protagonist in his own version of the world." ~John Rogers*

---

When you create your characters, spend the bulk of that time on their personality traits, as this will enable your characters to make their own decisions and lead the story down the path it needs to go, rather than you leading their journey.

Backstory molds the character's personality. Indiana Jones has a rich backstory that shapes his adulthood. The consummate adventurer, he had a knack at getting into trouble even as a child. One of those adventures left him with a phobia of snakes—a fear that he was forced to face as an adult.

Backstory contains the pivotal points in a character's life that shapes them. Were they abused or pampered? Did they grow up on a farm, in a city, or on a spaceship? Did they have parents, siblings, friends?

Once you have a few key details noted for each of your major characters, be sure to write them down. I create a biography for every character. The major characters often have several bullet points as well as a picture of an actor who I envision as them. Minor characters may have no more than a bullet point or two. At a minimum, I list the character's name, role within the story, key personality traits, and notable backstory. Often, I gain more insight into each character, such as pet peeves, as I write the book, and I fill in new details on the biographies as needed.

I intentionally spend very few words describing physical attributes of my characters and instead focus on what makes them tick. Sure, I'll point out any physical trait that is unique, such as a scar or a disability, but I leave it to my readers to envision the character in their own minds.

Creating your characters before starting your novel may take as little as an hour, but having real characters going in can save you tens, if not hundreds, of hours in writer's block and frustration. The better you understand your characters' mindset, strengths, and weaknesses, the faster they will take on lives of their own and drive out the story. That is, the more you let the characters run with the story, the less outlining you have to do.

## Step 4: Build a world that readers crave to visit

Worldbuilding is a crucial element of fantasy and historical fiction, but it's important to all stories. After all, the world you create is the world in which your characters to exist. If you write contemporary fiction, you have it easier than many since readers live in this world, but a good, three-dimensional setting is necessary in all novels. Readers may fall in love with characters, but through worldbuilding, you can transport readers away to brand new worlds.

Worldbuilding isn't long descriptions of the physical surroundings (although that's commonly found in epic fantasy); it's all the components of the world. Engaging all five senses—and moving deeper than physical attributes—will tug the reader's emotions. Unlike character development, don't be afraid to start writing your story with minimal details on your world. For any contemporary genre, you can work out many of the details once you start writing.

First, setting is crucial to all genres. When and where does your story take place? Does it take place today in London or two hundred years from now on Mars? Depending on the location you select, you may have a specific landmark, holiday, or natural disaster that you can incorporate into your story.

Once you know the location and time period, what is the emotion or mood you want to convey through the setting? If it's a murder mystery, you may start with an old, abandoned house. Or, if it's an edgy, young adult romance, you may open in a high school full of cliques. Many dystopian stories have dark, polluted skies that shadow the oppressors' dark actions.

Knowing the setting will guide you into the other details of your world. For example, if you're writing a historical fantasy, you'll need to develop snippets of its history. In paranormal stories, you'll want to pay special attention to mythology—the lore, legends, and religions. Different dialects or jargon may come into play in a space adventure. In a dystopia, the legal system, such as what's against the law and how people are punished, is important.

Culture is to worldbuilding as personalities are to characters. Culture shows the unique quirks of a particular place. Daily routines, traditions, taboos, attitudes, prejudices, and fashion can make your world a place that readers crave to visit, like a Quidditch match in Harry Potter. Or, culture can reveal a place so horrible that, like a bad accident, your readers are enthralled and can't look away…like any good horror story.

Having a general understanding on your world before you start writing puts your characters in a place that can help, hinder, or terrify them.

## Step 5: Have a roadmap and you won't get lost

Before you start writing, consider creating a high-level storyboard that serves as a guide for your story. A storyboard is a simple outline of major plot points, i.e., moments that impact the protagonist's journey. For my storyboards, I include the inciting incident (what gets the story started), conflicts, deaths, betrayals, and other key plot points. It rarely looks like an outline; it's more of a page with plot points jotted on it, and arrows leading from one plot point to another. Some plot points have no lines to or from them, because I don't yet know how they'll fit into the story. As I write my novel, I update the storyboard to reflect the scenes actually written, chapter by chapter. It makes both self-editing and the synopsis writing much easier.

Don't spend too much time on your storyboard. Once you begin writing, your characters will take over and lead you down paths you never expected.

Having a solid understanding of your story's premise, demographics, and characters will give you armor to blast through writer's block. Identifying your world and having a roadmap will help you write faster, which can help you stay in the groove as you write your novel.

THREE

## Write your novel confidently through Little Ups

---

---

"You can't write a novel all at once, any more than you can swallow a whale in one gulp. You do have to break it up into smaller chunks. But those smaller chunks aren't good old familiar short stories. Novels aren't built out of short stories. They are built out of scenes." ~ Orson Scott Card

---

Writing a novel is a personal process and should feel natural to you. That's why I don't prescribe writing a certain number of words per day or following a rigid outline. Instead, focus on achieving Little Ups, mini milestones so that you know you're making progress. Before each writing session—or if you like to schedule, before you begin writing—set Little Up goals. As mentioned earlier, pick goals that are realistic but also challenge you. After all, the Big Up is to finish the novel!

My Little Up goals are unique to the book I'm currently working on. I often set a goal to complete a particular scene in each writing session. Under a tight deadline, I've often set a goal to complete a chapter in each writing session.

I recommend setting at least one Little Up goal for each writing session. That way, once you accomplish the Little Up, you can treat yourself to a little celebration, which could be a break, a visit to social media, or taking a walk.

Little Ups work because they are tangible steps forward in writing a novel. When you're writing three hundred or more pages, it's easy to feel overwhelmed or lost. You've already done all the planning; now it's time to watch yourself make solid progress on your novel. It doesn't matter how small the Little Up is, as long as it propels you and your story.

If you're a plotter, you can set your Little Up goals before each writing session. If you're a planner, you can build a list of your Little Up goals up front and map them to dates so that you'll see when you'll finish your novel by achieving all your Little Ups. However you choose to define your Little Up goals, don't wait too long to start writing, or else you'll lose some excitement you built during the planning steps, and you'll likely forget some brainstorming you did.

Jump in and write, using Little Ups to boost motivation and celebrate your accomplishments along the way. The rest of this section gives tips on writing the beginning, the ending, and the challenging depths in between.

## Tip 1: The secret to the first (and last) scene

The first sentence and the first page of a novel get a lot of attention. They're what grab the readers' attention at the bookstore so that they buy your book. The first page can make the difference between an editor asking to see your full manuscript and passing on it. Yes, the first page is important, but that doesn't mean you have to get it perfect on the first draft.

My editor cut the first few pages on my first book because I'd started in the wrong place in the scene. I had spent dozens of hours on that first line. It was perfect. But my editor was right. The book was better for cutting it.

After over a dozen novels, I can say that the secret to the writing the first scene is to *just write it*. Start writing. Don't let perfection be a roadblock. It doesn't matter if the first scene is ugly—that's what first drafts are for. Once you write a couple chapters, or even the entire novel, you'll find that when you return to the first scene, it will become easier to polish it into a world-class introduction. By then, you'll have an intimate understanding of the inciting incident and how best to introduce your protagonist.

Whereas the first scene entices readers to buy your novel, the last scene entices readers to buy your *next* novel. The final scene can bog down writers trying to achieve perfection. Take the same approach with the ending as you do with the beginning. Just get it down and revise it after you've had a chance to read your novel end-to-end. Once you see the full story with fresh eyes, it'll be easier to refine your ending into a great, fulfilling wrap-up for your reader.

## Tip 2: Write the first draft without fear

*"This is how you do it: you sit down at the keyboard and you put one word after another until it's done. It's that easy, and that hard."* ~Neil Gaiman

Note that the heading to this tip refers to your "first draft," not simply your "draft." That's because you're not limited to writing one draft. Your story doesn't have to be perfect the first time. Your second draft is the opportunity to turn your *good* story into a *great* story.

A few writers, often the more experienced ones, write a single draft, and they self-edit along the way. They have an expert-level grasp of worldbuilding, character development, and the plot of their stories. If this is your first novel, don't try this, or else you may find yourself trying to constantly polish as you write. You'll be writing like you're riding a bike with the brakes on; you'll never find the momentum you need to finish the novel.

Some first-time novelists find themselves in this rut, and they take years to complete their novel because they're constantly rewriting and tweaking it as they write. They're writing backward, sideways, and every other direction except forward…the direction they need to go to reach the finish line.

Instead, give yourself permission to write ugly. I write a first draft that's often horribly rough. But, I have the end-to-end story on paper, which is so much easier to improve and polish on a second draft than to start with a blank page. By taking this approach, I don't allow myself to spend too much time on a scene or chapter, letting it become quicksand to my momentum. When I know I need to fill in plot holes or rework a scene, I note the changes needed and then move on to the next scene.

The key to finishing the first draft is to keep writing *forward*.

If you focus on moving ahead into the next scene, and the scene after that, you'll finish each writing session with a sense of accomplishment and energized to continue.

## Tip 3: Every draft after the first gets easier

There is no magic number as to how many times you should go through your novel. You may have it refined after two passes, or it may take five passes.

My first draft contains what I call the bones of the story. I focus on covering all the plot points and moving the story forward, but the story (typically) lacks depth.

Once that I have the full story on paper, I begin my second draft in which I add the meat to the story. I pay attention to the details, creating depth through narrative, dialogue, and deep point of view (POV) where it's needed. The second draft is also where I move around scenes or delete unnecessary content, such as the numbing "day in the life" scenes that make readers' eyes glaze over.

After finishing the first draft, you may want to send off your novel immediately, but I advise against it. By doing so, you may shortchange yourself and your story by not ensuring it's fully developed. Just like no one wants to eat a half-baked cake, no reader wants a half-baked story. Walk through your novel at least one more time to make sure it's complete and delivers a worthwhile read.

FOUR

## Life changes the moment you finish your novel

The moment you write, "The End," your life changes. You've written a novel! This is a huge accomplishment, and you should be very proud. You have a choice to make: you can keep the manuscript to yourself, or you can share it with the world. If you choose to put the manuscript in a drawer, there's nothing wrong with that. Not all books are meant for the outside world. However, if you choose to proceed with the publishing process, read on for more tips.

### Self-edit to make your novel stand out

In *The Tidy Guide to Self-Editing Your Novel*, I go into detail on how to self-edit your story so that it's so polished it shines. When you self-edit, you'll look at the story as a whole, which is called content editing or developmental editing. Then, you'll dive deep into each paragraph—this is called copy editing. Last, you'll put the final polish on by proofreading your manuscript, after which, you'll be ready to enter the publishing process with confidence.

## Prepare for the publishing process

Ready for the world to see your novel? Great! Here's where you have a big decision to make: What publishing route is a best fit for your novel? Today's publishing industry offers more opportunities than ever before. Self-publishing and traditional publishing are the two best-known paths, but they aren't your only options. You can also serialize your novel, posting one chapter at a time, on Wattpad. Dozens of breakout successes on Wattpad have been picked up by publishing houses and movie studios. Yours could become one of them.

There are pros and cons to each publishing path you choose. Traditional publishing often offers an up-front advance and guides you through the publishing process, but it can also be frustratingly slow—from finding an agent or editor through release often takes longer than a year.

Self-publishing can be much faster—you move at your own pace. You have complete control over every aspect of the process, but that means you bear full responsibility for every aspect and may incur some upfront costs for cover design, editing, and proofreading.

In *The Tidy Guide to Publishing Your Novel,* I cover publishing options in more detail and dig into each step to self-publishing your own novel.

## Start the next novel

Now that you've finished your novel, you can cross that goal off your bucket list and celebrate. What should you do now? Why not start writing the next novel? Writing your first book is hard work; writing your second book is a little bit easier. When writing the first novel, you begin to develop personal writing processes and habits that work for you. You learn what works and what doesn't for you as a writer. You can apply these lessons as you begin a second novel. With each subsequent novel you write, you'll find that you are writing better and faster as you gain expertise and experience.

## Believe in yourself and everything will turn out fine

Writing a novel isn't rocket science, but it's hard work...*really* hard work. Conveying a protagonist's journey in a cohesive series of plot points across hundreds of pages can feel overwhelming. Remind yourself that the first draft —or even the second draft—doesn't have to be perfect. Give yourself the freedom to write the words your fingers want to type. Trust your mind, and the story will come together. You may even discover that you're meant to be a novelist!

---

## Message from the author:

This is the first Tidy Guide in a series of 30-minute reads that will cover writing, editing, publishing, and marketing books and managing your authorial career.

If you would take two minutes to post a review, I would be very grateful. If you write a review, please email me at Rachel@RachelAukes.com and I will add you to a list of advance readers for the next book in the series. You will receive a free early e-copy in return for an online review.

Also by Rachel Aukes

**The Tidy Guides Series** (Nonfiction)

*The Tidy Guide to Writing a Novel*

*The Tidy Guide to Self-Editing Your Novel*

**Fringe Series**

*Fringe Runner*

*Fringe Station*

*Fringe Campaign*

*Fringe War*

*Fringe Legacy*

**Colliding Worlds Trilogy**

*Collision*

*Implosion*

*Explosion*

**The Deadland Saga**

*100 Days in Deadland*

*Deadland's Harvest*

*Deadland Rising*

**Standalone Fiction**

*Stealing Fate*

# About the Author

Rachel Aukes is the award-winning author of *100 Days in Deadland*, which made Suspense Magazine's Best of the Year list. She is also a Wattpad Star, her stories having over five million reads. When not writing, she can be found flying old airplanes across the Midwest countryside and catering to an exceptionally spoiled fifty-pound lapdog.

Join Rachel's readers club to get early access to new releases, sign up for contests, and receive free stuff:
www.rachelaukes.com/newsletter

www.ingramcontent.com/pod-product-compliance
Lightning Source LLC
Chambersburg PA
CBHW051040030426
42336CB00015B/2970